*Viva Chocolate!*

Rio Nuevo Publishers®
P.O. Box 5250, Tucson, Arizona 85703-0250
(520) 623-9558, www.rionuevo.com

Text and photography © 2008 by Rio Nuevo Publishers. Food styling
by Tracy Vega.

Photography credits as follows:
W. Ross Humphreys: page 74.
Robin Stancliff: front and back covers, pages 3, 4, 5, 14, 17, 19, 20, 24,
29, 32, 35, 37, 43, 50, 55, 68.

Library of Congress Cataloging-in-Publication Data

Noble, Marilyn.
Viva chocolate! / by Marilyn Noble.
Includes index.
    p. cm. — (Cook west series)
ISBN 978-1-933855-10-3
1. Cookery (Chocolate) 2. Chocolate. I. Title.
TX767.C5N62 2007
641.6'374—dc22

                    2007024560



Design: Karen Schober, Seattle, Washington.
Printed in Korea.


10 9 8 7 6 5 4 3 2 1

# *viva* chocolate!

**MARILYN NOBLE**

RIO NUEVO PUBLISHERS
TUCSON, ARIZONA

COOK WEST
SERIES

# contents

Introduction  **6**

**The Basics  14**

**The Perfect Wake–Up
Call  17**

**Everyday Pastries and
Snacks  24**

**It's What's
for Dinner  32**

**Sweet Dreams  37**

**Daring Drinks  68**

Appendix I: Working
with Chocolate  **75**

Appendix II: Resources  **77**

Index  **78**

When you tell people your next project is a chocolate cook-book, you get two reactions. The first is usually an enthusiastic offer to be a taste-tester, and the second is the gift of a favorite chocolate recipe. Part of chocolate's mythology is the fact that most people in the Western world enjoy it, and many are obsessed with it. That's been the case for centuries, since the days of the Emperor Montezuma, who was rumored to drink fifty cups of chocolate a day.

Chocolate is not only a sweet treat—in the Southwest and throughout Mexico and Central America, cocoa flavors meat-based main dishes, like *mole*, a savory, spicy sauce that lends a kick to roasted meats. Chocolate is a perfect foil for coffee drinks, and if you've never experienced the heady sensation of a nibble of premium bittersweet chocolate with a sip of Grand Echezeaux from Burgundy, your gastronomical adventures aren't yet complete.

In this collection of recipes, you'll find my favorites, as well as some from my chocolate-obsessed friends. Some are classics with a twist to give them a Southwestern flavor, others are elegant creations that will impress your dinner guests, and some are simple, everyday indulgences for the kids—or for anybody else who suffers the craving that can only be satisfied with a chocolate overload.

The Classic Period Mayans (A.D. 250–900) were the first known civilization to cultivate cacao, a wild tree from the rain forests of South America. The Mayans fermented, roasted, and ground the beans much as we do today; but without modern machinery to process it further, they didn't enjoy the smooth, creamy chocolate bars that we know. Instead, chocolate was a drink made with the bitter ground beans and water, and flavored with chile, vanilla, black pepper, and cornmeal. The only sweetening may have been a touch of honey. The unheated liquid was poured back and forth between jars until it was frothy and ready to drink.

The Mayans consumed chocolate for medicinal purposes and as a part of rituals, such as weddings, and the beans were often offered to the gods. Chocolate was a treat, but imbibing didn't depend on social station. Everyone was entitled to a cup now and then.

As the Aztec civilization rose to power in Mexico, the Aztecs began trading with the Mayans, and cacao beans became the currency of choice. Because the Aztecs couldn't cultivate the trees in the dry central Mexican highlands, the beans became precious. In Aztec society, only the wealthy and royalty were allowed and could afford to drink chocolate. For everyone else, it was used as money, more valuable for paying tribute or for trading for food, clothing, and household goods than for drinking.

### A BRIEF HISTORY OF CHOCOLATE

When the Spaniard Hernán Cortés conquered the Aztecs in 1521, he carried cacao beans back to Spain. Spaniards quickly became enamored of the bitter drink but began to sweeten it with sugar and cinnamon and add milk. Eventually, the chocolate craze swept through the royal houses of Europe, and soon the French, British, Dutch, and Spanish were developing cacao plantations in the New World.

For 200 years, chocolate remained a drink for society's elite, prized for its medicinal and restorative properties. The Industrial Revolution, however, changed the way the world experienced chocolate. Wind- and steam-driven mills made it easier and cheaper to grind the beans and produce chocolate in large quantities, and in 1828, Dutch chemist Coenraad Van Houten invented the cocoa press, which separated chocolate into its components—cocoa butter and the solids left behind, known as cocoa presscake. Cocoa presscake, when crumbled, became cocoa powder. In 1847, the chocolate bar was born when a company in England, Fry's, discovered a way to mix cocoa, melted cocoa butter, and sugar into a paste. In 1875, Henri Nestlé combined chocolate with milk powder to create milk chocolate, an instant sensation. In 1879, Rodolphe Lindt invented conching, a way of kneading the chocolate paste for an extended period of time to smooth out the flavor and reduce acidity. In 1894, Milton Hershey introduced the first mass-produced chocolate bars to the world, and for the next 100 years, chocolate was a mainstay treat of the masses.

About twenty years ago, with advances in food science and technology, a new breed of chocolatier arrived on the scene. These mostly small, boutique companies create artisanal chocolate bars using beans grown on their own plantations and processed under exacting conditions. As with fine wine and coffee, consumers can now become refined tasters, understanding the nuances of flavor and aroma that come with different varieties of beans, growing regions, and combinations of ingredients.

Cacao trees (*Theobroma cacao*) have a relatively small growing range, between 20 degrees of latitude north and south of the equator, in tropical rainforests. The trees are picky, needing partial shade, regular moisture, constant high humidity, and warm temperatures. In addition to its native South American habitat, cacao is cultivated in Central America, the Caribbean, Indonesia, and Africa. In fact, Ivory Coast and Ghana produce 70 percent of the world's cacao beans.

**THE LONG JOURNEY FROM BEAN TO BAR**

The trees produce pods—gnarled fruit that grows close to the lower branches and trunk, requiring hand harvesting. Inside, each pod holds thirty to fifty beans wrapped in a sweet pulp. After the pods are picked, workers with machetes split the pods and place the beans and pulp in boxes that they then cover with banana leaves. The beans ferment for three to seven days until the pulp liquefies and drains away, leaving behind brown beans containing the precursors of the rich chocolate flavor that will continue to develop as the process continues.

Next, the beans are dried, either on open-air trays in the sun or on racks with hot, forced air. Once they reach about 6 percent moisture, they're packed in burlap bags for shipping to market, where they're inspected by buyers for the chocolate manufacturers of the world.

Once the beans reach the manufacturer, they are sorted, cleaned, and weighed before roasting, much like coffee beans. After roasting, the beans enter a machine that cracks the seed coats and blows them away, leaving behind cocoa nibs, the broken pieces of roasted cacao beans that are winnowed according to size. The nibs contain 47 percent cocoa solids and 53 percent cocoa butter. They are milled into a peanut butter-like paste called chocolate liquor.

Some chocolate liquor is pressed, to separate the cocoa butter and the cocoa solids. The cocoa butter, when added back to chocolate liquor, creates "fine" chocolate, which is stable at room temperature. It can also be added to cocoa powder, along with milk, sugar, and other flavorings, to create mass-market chocolate. Cocoa butter is also used in cosmetics and other household products. The cocoa solids are pulverized into cocoa powder.

When chocolate liquor is blended with cocoa butter, and/or sugar, vanilla, milk, and an emulsifier such as lecithin, it becomes a dry, gritty mixture known as "crumb." The crumb is refined by sending it through a series of stainless steel rollers to break down the particles, resulting in a smoother end product. The resulting paste is then "conched"—kneaded and aerated for several days to improve the texture and allow the excess acids and moisture to evaporate.

The final step is "tempering," a careful heating and cooling of the chocolate to create a stable crystalline structure. Tempered chocolate is glossy, has a smooth texture, and breaks sharply. Poorly tempered chocolate can be grainy and waxy or powdery. Finally, the chocolate becomes the end product—molded bars, filled candies, or liquid flavoring to be added to other manufactured products such as ice cream.

**TYPES OF CHOCOLATE**

Just about everybody has a favorite chocolate, whether it's a bag of kisses or a chunk of single-estate, 70 percent dark chocolate. When cooking with chocolate, remember that the finished product, in many cases, will possess the same flavor, richness, and complexity as the chocolate you use to prepare the dish. Always use what tastes best to you. If you like grocery-store cocoa powder and baking chocolate, which is what most of us grew up tasting, you'll enjoy a cake or mousse made with them. If you want to get more adventurous, however, don't be afraid to experiment with premium, boutique chocolates. That same chocolate mousse reaches a new dimension when you make it with a fine chocolate. Not every recipe benefits from the extra expense of high-quality chocolate, however. In this book, if a recipe will be improved by using premium chocolate, the instructions will indicate it.

*Unsweetened chocolate.* Made from 100 percent cocoa liquor, unsweetened chocolate is bitter and cannot be used in place of bittersweet or semisweet chocolate. It is generally used only in cooking.

*Bittersweet, semisweet, or dark chocolate.* In the U.S., dark chocolate can contain no milk powder and must have a minimum of 35 percent cocoa solids. Most better brands contain much more than that, and the label reflects the percentage of cocoa liquor. The percentage of sugar usually determines whether a bar is bittersweet or semisweet. The higher the chocolate liquor percentage, the more pronounced the chocolate flavor, but each manufacturer has a signature that may appeal to different tasters in different ways. For most of the recipes in this book, bittersweet and semisweet chocolates are interchangeable. Discover what you like, and use it (and eat it) with abandon.

*Milk chocolate.* In the U.S., milk chocolate contains at least 10 percent chocolate liquor and 12 percent milk solids. It also contains a higher percentage of sugar than dark chocolate. While it's the most popular for eating, it's not used as much in baking.

*White chocolate.* Not really chocolate, white chocolate is made from cocoa butter, sugar, and flavorings. Since it isn't chocolate, you won't find many recipes in this book that call for white chocolate.

*Gianduia* (jon-DOO-ya). The Italians combined chocolate and hazelnut in a spread form, the most famous of which is Nutella. Pietro Ferrero, a pastry maker in Italy during World War II, created the product to extend the availability of chocolate, in short supply due to rationing. Today, Nutella outsells all brands of peanut butter combined. Other companies also make similar spreads.

*Chocolate chips.* Designed to hold their shape during the baking process, chocolate chips come in milk, dark, and white chocolate. Because they have a different cocoa butter content, I don't recommend using them in the place of bar chocolate in these recipes.

*Cocoa powder.* Pulverized solid that is left after the cocoa butter is removed from chocolate liquor, it comes unsweetened in two varieties, regular unprocessed cocoa powder and Dutch process. The latter is alkalized to neutralize the acid. They have very different tastes and react differently in baked goods. When using baking *soda,* use unprocessed powder, and when using baking *powder,* use Dutch process. In this book, if a recipe calls for a specific type, it will specify it. Otherwise, use whichever appeals to your taste buds.

*Mexican chocolate.* While not considered as refined and superior as its European and American cousins, Mexican chocolate is essential to the flavor of many Mexican recipes. It's sweetened and flavored with cinnamon and comes in tablets that should be grated before using. Ibarra and Abuelita are popular brands found in many grocery stores.

**A NOTE ABOUT CHILE POWDERS**

Some of the recipes in this book call for different types of *chile* (not "chili") powders. The most common is made of dried and ground ancho chiles. It comes in different heats—use whichever your palate prefers. Pasilla, or chile negro, is commonly used in moles. Chipotle powder is made from dried smoked jalapeños and lends smoky heat to dishes, while habanero powder is fiery hot. If a recipe doesn't specify a particular type, use the best ancho powder you can find, usually from New Mexico. Just make sure that you use pure chile powder. Many brands you find in the grocery store are actually blends of cumin, salt, and garlic powder in addition to the chile powder, and will make a dramatic difference in the taste of the dish. (See Appendix II for sources.)

**TOASTING NUTS**

Many of the recipes in this collection call for toasted almonds, pecans, piñons, or walnuts. Toasting brings out the sweetness of the nuts and concentrates their flavor. It's an easy process, whether you do it in the oven or in a skillet. To toast in the oven, preheat to 400 degrees F. Spread the nuts in a single layer on a baking sheet and bake for 5–8 minutes, shaking once halfway through the cooking time. To toast in a skillet, spread a single layer of nuts and toast over high heat, shaking the skillet frequently, for about 3–5 minutes. In either case, you'll know they're done when the nuts are fragrant and light brown.

*The Basics*
xxxxxx

# Basic Chocolate Sauce

xxxxxx

*Use the best chocolate you can afford, because flavor is every-thing in a chocolate sauce. Experiment with variations by adding espresso powder, mint, rum, or fruit flavorings. If you need a quick dessert, a store-bought pound cake, some berries, and a little of this sauce will impress even the most critical foodie.*

*Makes about 2 cups*

**8 ounces premium bittersweet chocolate, finely chopped**

**1 cup heavy cream**

**½ cup light corn syrup**

Place the chopped chocolate in a heat-proof bowl. Heat the heavy cream and corn syrup in a saucepan over medium heat until it begins to simmer. Remove from heat and pour half of this mixture over the chocolate. Let it sit for 1 minute, then whisk until the chocolate is melted. Add the remaining cream-mixture and stir to blend. A handheld immersion blender helps to incorporate the melted chocolate into the cream mixture. Store in the refrigerator for up to 2 weeks. To serve, warm in the microwave.

# Basic Ganache

xxxxxx

*Ganache is an elegant cake frosting and is the building block of truffles. Again, use good chocolate and experiment with fla-vorings.*

*Makes about 3 cups*

**16 ounces premium bittersweet chocolate, finely chopped**

**1½ cups heavy cream**

Place the chopped chocolate in a heatproof bowl. Heat the cream until simmering, then remove from heat and pour about ½ cup over the chocolate. Stir until melted and add remaining cream. Use a handheld immersion blender for the best results.

Alternate method: Place chunks of chocolate in the bowl of a food processor. Process until pulverized. With the machine running, pour in the hot cream in a steady stream. Process until the chocolate is melted.

Allow to cool at room temperature. If not using immediately, store tightly covered in the refrigerator for up to 2 weeks.

### Basic Chocolate Syrup

xxxxxx

*Makes about 1½ cups*

1 cup water
¾ cup sugar
1 cup cocoa powder
1 teaspoon vanilla extract

*Experiment with different cocoas until you find the most pleasing to you. This syrup is great for sundaes, pancakes, or stirred into a mug of hot milk for a quick and easy hot chocolate. Chocolate syrup is a low-fat alternative to chocolate sauce, which is made with cream and so has a richer texture and taste.*

Place the water and sugar in a saucepan and bring to a boil over medium heat, stirring until the sugar is dissolved. Immediately whisk in the cocoa powder, stirring until dissolved. Cook until thickened. Remove the mixture from the heat, allow it to cool slightly, and then stir in the vanilla. Refrigerate tightly covered for up to 2 weeks.

## Chocolate Chip Pecan Pancakes

xxxxxx

*Serves 4*

1½ cups flour

3 tablespoons sugar

1 tablespoon baking powder

¼ teaspoon salt

2 eggs

1¼ cups milk

½ teaspoon vanilla extract

3 tablespoons unsalted butter, melted, plus more for griddle if needed

½ cup chopped pecans

½ cup semisweet chocolate chips

Confectioners' sugar, for garnish

Basic Chocolate Syrup, warm or at room temperature (see page 16)

*When I was a kid, our favorite breakfast was chocolate chip pancakes. The chocolate chips get crunchy on the outside and gooey on the inside.*

In a large bowl, combine the flour, sugar, baking powder, and salt. In a separate bowl, beat the eggs, and then stir in the milk and vanilla. Stir in the melted butter. Add the egg mixture to the dry ingredients, stirring just until the batter is thick. Lumps are fine. Avoid over-mixing.

Preheat a griddle and brush it with melted butter. Pour ¼ cup of batter onto the surface of the griddle for each pancake. As soon as the batter sets a little, sprinkle with pecans and chocolate chips. When bubbles come to the surface, flip the pancakes and cook for approximately 1 more minute. Remove to serving plates, dust lightly with confectioners' sugar, and drizzle with warm chocolate syrup.

# Gianduia Puff Pastry

xxxxxx

*This resembles a giant cheese Danish, so it's perfect for break-fast, but it makes a nice dinner dessert as well.*

Preheat oven to 350 degrees F. On a flour-covered surface, roll out 1 sheet of puff pastry until thin. Trim into a 9-inch circle and place on a large ungreased cookie sheet. From the leftover scraps of puff pastry, cut decorative shapes such as leaves to garnish the top. Set aside.

In a small bowl, mix the gianduia with 3 tablespoons of half-and-half until it reaches a spreading consistency. Smooth over the puff pastry circle, leaving a 1-inch margin.

In another small bowl, mix the ricotta, egg, and additional half-and-half until it reaches a spreading consistency. Smooth over the gianduia.

Roll out the remaining puff pastry and trim it into 9-inch cir-cle. Combine the egg yolk with the milk until blended. Brush a small amount around the edge of the bottom pastry, then place the remaining pastry circle on top of the ricotta, sealing the edges and crimping. Brush the top with the remaining egg wash. Place "leaves" or other pastry designs in a decorative pattern on the top.

Bake 30 minutes or until the pastry is golden brown. Remove from oven, cool slightly, and sift cocoa powder and sugar over the top. Serve warm, cut into wedges.

*Serves 6*

**Flour**

**1 package (2 sheets) frozen puff pastry, thawed**

**1 cup gianduia spread, such as Nutella**

**3 tablespoons half-and-half**

**1 cup ricotta**

**1 egg**

**3 tablespoons half-and-half**

**1 egg yolk**

**2 tablespoons milk**

**2 tablespoons cocoa powder, for garnish**

**2 tablespoons confectioners' sugar, for garnish**

## Chocolate Stuffed French Toast with Orange Marmalade Sauce

xxxxxx

*Serves 6*

12 one-inch-thick slices French bread, slightly dry

Butter for pan

1⅛ cups sugar

⅔ cups cocoa powder

2 cups milk

6 eggs, lightly beaten

2 teaspoons vanilla extract

2 cartons (8 ounces each) mascarpone

4 ounces bittersweet chocolate, grated

½ cup orange marmalade

½ cup orange juice

*For an elegant brunch, serve with mimosas. Note that you will need to prepare this dish several hours before you plan to cook it.*

Place 6 slices of French bread in a buttered 9 x 13-inch pan.

In a large mixing bowl, combine the sugar and cocoa powder until well blended. Add the milk, beaten eggs, and vanilla, stirring until the mixture is well blended. Pour half of the egg mixture over the French bread in the pan, making sure that the pieces are completely coated.

In a separate bowl, stir the mascarpone until smooth, then spread it over the bread. Sprinkle mascarpone with grated chocolate. Top with the remaining 6 pieces of bread, and then pour the remaining egg mixture over all. Cover the pan with foil and refrigerate 8 hours or overnight.

Remove the dish from the refrigerator and allow to sit at room temperature for 30 minutes. Preheat oven to 350 degrees F. Bake, covered, for 55–60 minutes. Remove from the oven and let sit for about 5 minutes.

After the French toast comes out of the oven, melt the orange marmalade in a saucepan and add the orange juice. Simmer until reduced and thickened. Serve warm with the French toast.

# Double Chocolate Cherry Muffins

xxxxxx

*These dense, rich muffins are a chocolate addict's delight.*

*Makes 12*

Preheat oven to 400 degrees F. Butter 12 muffin tins or line with paper muffin cups.

In a heavy saucepan over medium heat, melt together the butter, chocolate, and milk, stirring constantly. When the chocolate is completely melted, remove from heat and cool for 15 minutes.

In a separate bowl combine the flour, cocoa powder, sugar, baking powder, baking soda, and salt until well-mixed. When the chocolate mixture has cooled, whisk the two eggs until lightly beaten and then add to the chocolate mixture, whisking until thoroughly blended. Add the chocolate mixture to the dry ingredients, stirring until the batter is mixed. Don't over-stir; some lumps will remain. Stir the cherries and chocolate chips into the mixture, then spoon the mixture into the pre-pared muffin tins.

Bake 14–18 minutes or until a tester inserted comes out clean. Serve warm. Keep leftovers in a tightly sealed bag for up to 3 days.

**6 tablespoons butter, plus more for muffin tins**

**4 ounces bittersweet chocolate, coarsely chopped**

**1 cup milk**

**1⅓ cups flour**

**⅓ cup cocoa powder**

**1½ cups brown sugar**

**1½ teaspoons baking powder**

**½ teaspoon baking soda**

**½ teaspoon salt**

**2 eggs**

**1 cup dried tart cherries**

**1 cup semisweet chocolate chips**

# *Everyday Pastries and Snacks*

xxxxxx

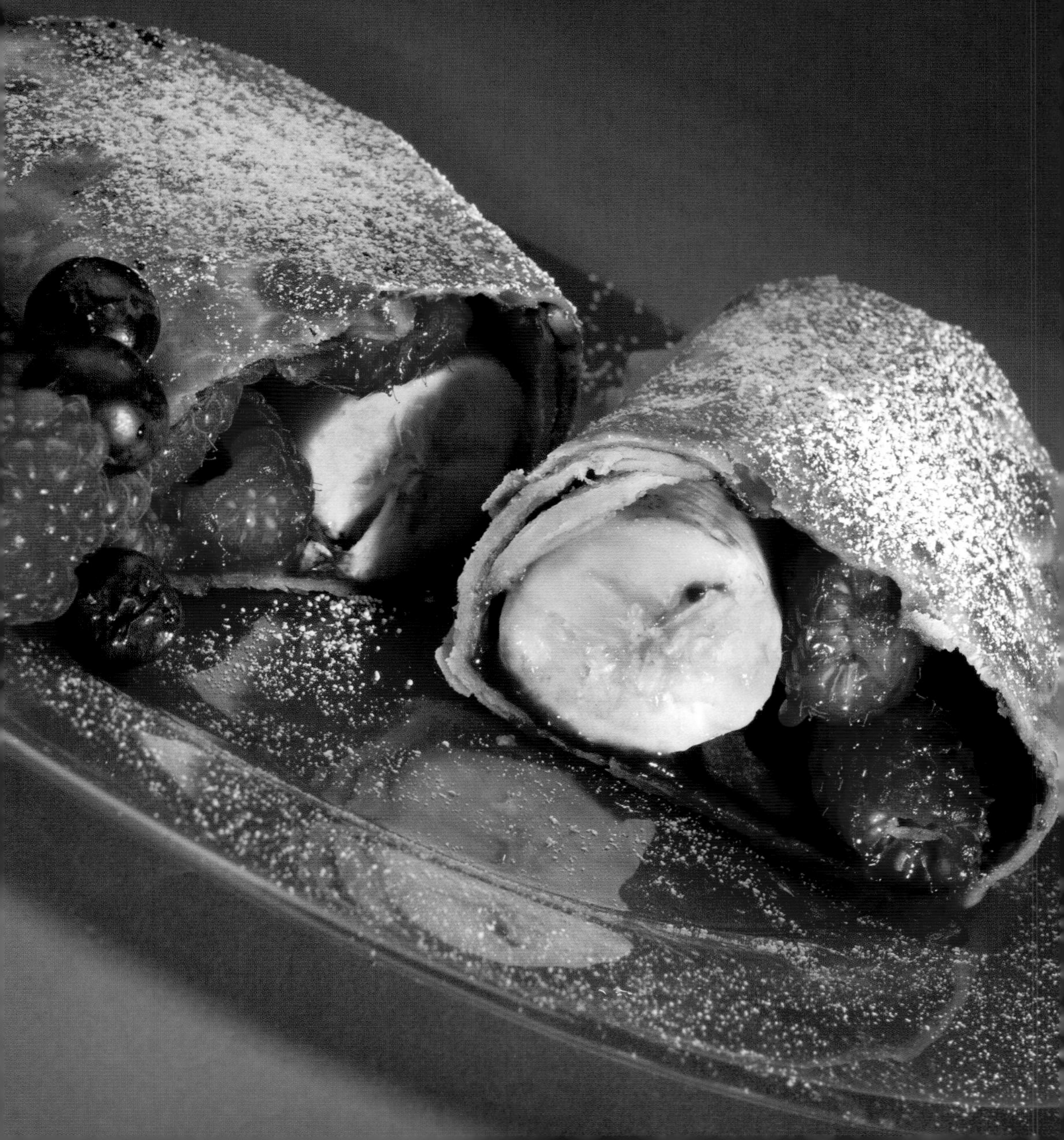

## Chocolate Burritos

xxxxxx

*A light and fun dessert after a Mexican dinner.*

*Serves 4*

On a heated griddle, warm the flour tortillas until soft. Spread 2 tablespoons of gianduia on each tortilla. Place a peeled banana at the edge of 1 tortilla, then top with one-quarter of the raspberries. Fold in the edges and roll burrito style. Repeat for the other 3 tortillas.

Melt the butter on the griddle and place the burritos, seam-side down, on the griddle. Brown lightly, then turn and brown the other side. Remove from heat. Cut each burrito diagonally across the middle, place on serving plates, and sprinkle with confectioners' sugar. Serve immediately.

**4 flour tortillas (10-inch size)**

**½ cup gianduia spread, such as Nutella**

**4 bananas**

**1 pint fresh raspberries, washed and blotted dry**

**2 tablespoons butter**

**Confectioners' sugar, for garnish**

## Chocolate Pizza

xxxxxx

*Sculptor Reno Carollo, whose middle name could be "Abbon-danza," created this abundance of chocolate and nuts. It's always a big hit with the kids and their parents, too.*

*Serves 12*

Preheat oven to 375 degrees F. In a food processor, grind the cookies until coarse crumbs remain, then add the melted butter and blend. Spray a pizza pan with cooking spray, and then press in the cookie mix to form a crust. Bake for 8 minutes. Remove from the oven and allow to cool slightly.

Spread gianduia over the warm crust, covering completely. Pour on a layer of melted jam, and then cover with white and

**30 chocolate sandwich cookies, such as Oreos**

**6 tablespoons melted butter**

**Cooking spray**

**1 cup gianduia spread, such as Nutella**

**½ cup raspberry jam, melted**

**½ cup white chocolate chips**

**½ cup semisweet chocolate chips**

**½ cup chopped pecans**

semisweet chocolate chips and pecans. Return to the oven and bake for about 10 minutes or until the chocolate chips melt slightly. Remove from the oven and cool for about 5 minutes and then, using a pizza cutter, slice into wedges. Serve warm. For an added sugar rush, top with a scoop of vanilla ice cream.

### Grilled Chocolate–Peanut-Butter Sandwiches
xxxxx

*Serves 4*

4 slices challah bread

¼ cup peanut butter

4 ounces bittersweet chocolate

2 teaspoons butter

Confectioners' sugar, for garnish

*My friend Heidi Bergos says her daughter loves these, and who wouldn't? It's almost like eating a grilled peanut-butter cup.*

On each of 2 slices of bread, spread a layer of peanut butter. Top each with 2 ounces of chocolate, then top with the remaining bread. Heat a skillet until a drop of water sizzles, and then butter both sides of each sandwich and place in the skillet. Turning once, cook until the bread is golden brown on both sides and the chocolate and peanut butter are melting on the inside. Remove from the skillet, slice in half diagonally, and dust with confectioners' sugar.

## Chocolate Pumpkin Empanadas

XXXXXX

*When I was growing up, pumpkin empanadas were a staple in our house, because my mother's friend Anna always made them for us. Adding a little chocolate turns them into a super-comfort food.*

Sift together the flour, baking powder, sugar, and salt. Cut in the butter until the mixture resembles coarse meal. Add the milk, a tablespoon at a time, until the dough is soft and holds together. Wrap the dough in plastic and refrigerate for 30 minutes.

Preheat the oven to 350 degrees F.

In a large bowl, combine the pumpkin, condensed milk, egg, cinnamon, ginger, and nutmeg until well blended. Roll out the dough on a floured board to about ⅛-inch thickness. Cut into 4-inch circles. In the center of each circle, place about 2 table-spoons of filling and top with a piece of chocolate. Fold the crust over, forming a semicircle, and seal the edges using a little water and a fork to crimp. Place on an ungreased baking sheet and brush the top of each empanada with a little beaten egg, then sprinkle with a little sugar.

Bake for 45 minutes or until golden brown. Serve warm.

*Makes about 16*

3 cups flour

2 teaspoons baking powder

3 tablespoons sugar

½ teaspoon salt

½ cup butter, very cold and cut into pieces

¼ cup milk

1 can (15 ounces) pumpkin (not pie filling)

1 can (14 ounces) sweetened condensed milk

1 egg

1 teaspoon ground cinnamon

½ teaspoon ginger

½ teaspoon ground nutmeg

8 ounces premium dark chocolate, broken into 16 uniform pieces

1 egg, beaten

¼ cup sugar

## Marbled Double Chocolate Chip Cookies

xxxxxx

*Makes about 5 dozen*

2¼ cups flour

1 teaspoon baking soda

1 teaspoon salt

1 cup unsalted butter, at room temperature

¾ cup granulated sugar

¾ cup firmly packed brown sugar

1 teaspoon vanilla extract

2 eggs

4 ounces bittersweet chocolate, finely chopped

2 cups semisweet chocolate chips

1 cup chopped pecans

*These started out as an accident when I was about 12 and left the flour out of the dough. The cookies melted together on the cookie sheet, and my mom scraped them back into the bowl. The melted chocolate chips created a nice marbled effect in the finished cookies. These are a bit easier to make.*

Preheat the oven to 375 degrees F. Combine the flour, baking soda, and salt in a small bowl. In a large bowl, cream together the butter, granulated sugar, brown sugar, and vanilla until light and fluffy. Beat in the eggs one at a time. Stir in the flour mixture until the dough is stiff and combined.

Melt the bittersweet chocolate (see Appendix I) and pour it into the bowl with the dough. Add the chocolate chips and pecans, stirring until barely mixed. The melted chocolate should swirl through the dough and create a marbled effect. Drop by teaspoons onto an ungreased baking sheet. Bake for about 10 minutes or until the cookies are golden-brown.

Remove from the oven. Remove the cookies from the baking sheet and allow to cool on a wire rack. Store in a tightly covered container.

## Chocolate Piñon Biscochitos

xxxxxx

*Makes 5 dozen*

1 pound pure lard

1 cup sugar

2 eggs

2 teaspoons aniseed, slightly crushed

6 cups flour

¼–½ cup brandy

16 ounces semisweet chocolate, finely chopped

1½ cups finely chopped piñons

*My friend Bill LeRoy is an adventurous cook and storyteller. He owns Elk Run Trading Company, a specialty food company known for its flavored marshmallows. His recipe for biscochitos, the state cookie of New Mexico, is an elegant twist on a classic. While some cooks use butter instead of lard, Bill says for the lightest cookie, you have to use the lard.*

Preheat the oven to 350 degrees F. In a large bowl, cream the lard until fluffy. Gradually add the sugar, beating constantly. Add the eggs one at a time, beating well after each addition. Stir in the aniseed. Mix in the flour by hand, and sprinkle in the brandy, using enough to make a soft dough. Let stand for about 10 minutes.

On a lightly floured board, roll out the dough to about ¼-inch thickness and cut into 3-inch circles. Bake for 15 minutes on ungreased cookie sheets. Remove from the cookie sheets and transfer to a wire rack while hot.

Melt the chocolate (see Appendix I) and pour the chopped piñons onto a sheet of waxed paper. Dip each cookie halfway into the chocolate and then into the nuts. Place on a wire rack to harden. Store in a single layer, tightly covered, for up to 1 week.

# Espresso Brownies

xxxxxx

*A cake-style brownie with the rich flavor of coffee to add complexity.*

Preheat oven to 350 degrees F. Grease an 8-inch-square baking pan.

In a small bowl, sift together the flour, baking powder, and espresso powder. In a large mixing bowl, cream the butter, sugar, and corn syrup until light and fluffy. Beat in the eggs one at a time. Stir in the liqueur and milk, blending just until mixed.

Melt the chocolate (see Appendix I) and add to the batter. Stir in the dry ingredients and add the walnuts. Pour the batter into the prepared pan and bake for about 20–30 minutes. Cool the brownies in the pan for about 10 minutes, then run a knife around the edges and invert the pan onto a rack to remove.

When completely cool, cut into 2-inch squares. Store in a tightly closed container.

*Makes 16*

½ cup flour

½ teaspoon baking powder

1 teaspoon espresso powder

¼ cup unsalted butter, at room temperature

¾ cup sugar

4 teaspoons light corn syrup

2 eggs, at room temperature

1 tablespoon coffee liqueur, such as Kahlúa

¼ cup milk, at room temperature

4 ounces unsweetened chocolate, finely chopped

1 cup chopped walnuts

*It's What's for Dinner*

xxxxx

# Pecan Chile Chicken
xxxxxx

*The sauce is rich and works well with rice and steamed asparagus on the side.*

With a mallet, gently pound the chicken breasts to a consistent thickness and set aside. Combine the pecans, chile powder, cocoa powder, garlic granules, cumin, pepper, and salt in a plastic zipper bag and shake until well blended. Add the chicken breasts one at a time and shake until coated.

Heat the olive oil in a deep skillet until hot, then add the prepared chicken breasts. Sauté about 2–3 minutes, then turn and sauté about another minute or 2. It's important not to overcook. Remove the chicken to a serving platter and tent with foil to keep warm.

Add butter to the skillet and scrape the bottom of the pan while it melts. Add the half-and-half, salt, and pecans, then heat until slightly reduced and thick. Pour this sauce over the chicken to serve.

*Serves 6*

6 boneless, skinless chicken breasts

½ cup finely ground pecans

2 tablespoons chile powder

2 tablespoons cocoa powder

1 tablespoon garlic granules

1 teaspoon ground cumin

1 teaspoon pepper

½ teaspoon salt

2 teaspoons olive oil

2 tablespoons butter

½ cup half-and-half

½ teaspoon salt

½ cup chopped pecans

## Smokin' Hot Chili

xxxxxx

*Serves 6*

2 tablespoons olive oil

½ cup all-purpose flour

1 teaspoon salt

½ teaspoon pepper

3 pounds sirloin, cut into 1-inch cubes

1 large onion, diced

6 cloves garlic, minced

1 cup New Mexico chile powder

3 tablespoons chipotle powder

¼ cup cocoa powder

1 teaspoon salt

1 teaspoon ground cumin

2 cans (14 ounces each) chopped tomatoes

6 cups beef broth

*Super Bowl Sunday will never be the same if you serve this spicy concoction. Who wants to watch the halftime show when you can eat this instead? Serve with a pan of cornbread and plenty of beer.*

Heat the olive oil in a Dutch oven. Combine the flour, salt, and pepper in a plastic zipper bag and add the sirloin in small batches, shaking to coat evenly. Add the coated sirloin to the hot oil and cook in batches over medium-high heat until browned. Remove meat from the pan and add the onion and garlic, stirring and scraping the bottom of the pan until the onions are soft and translucent, about 5 minutes.

Return the meat to the pan and add the chile powder, chipotle powder, cocoa powder, salt, and cumin. Stir to coat the meat and onions. Add the tomatoes and beef broth. Reduce heat, cover, and simmer for 2 hours.

# Chile-Rubbed Steaks

xxxxxx

*The cocoa powder adds a nice tang. Be sure to use pure chile powder, preferably from New Mexico. Serve with a hearty green salad and some grilled vegetables.*

Combine the chile powder, cocoa powder, paprika, cayenne, cumin, pepper, and salt in a small bowl until well blended. Rub into each steak until coated. Grill over high heat to desired doneness.

*Serves 4*

3 tablespoons chile powder

1 tablespoon cocoa powder

1 tablespoon paprika

1 teaspoon cayenne pepper

1 teaspoon ground cumin

1 teaspoon pepper

½ teaspoon salt

4 New York strip steaks (6 ounces each)

# Turkey Mole

xxxxxx

*Serves 6–8*

½ cup blanched almonds

4 tablespoons sesame seeds

1 tablespoon olive oil

1 ripe plantain (skin should be almost black), sliced

2 tablespoons ancho chile powder

2 tablespoons pasilla chile powder

2 tablespoons chipotle powder

2 teaspoons ground cinnamon

1 teaspoon salt

4 corn tortillas, shredded

1 small onion, diced

6 cloves garlic

4 ripe tomatoes, peeled and seeded

6 cups chicken broth

1 tablet Mexican chocolate, grated

1 turkey breast, about 3–5 pounds

*The origins of mole are somewhat murky, but nowadays you'll find as many different versions as there are cooks.*

Preheat oven to 350 degrees F. Spread the blanched almonds on a baking sheet and place in the oven. Roast until browned, stirring occasionally. Set aside. Reduce the oven temperature to 325 degrees F.

In a small sauté pan, heat the sesame seeds, stirring several times until golden brown. Set aside. In the same pan, heat the olive oil and add the slices of plantain. Sauté until soft.

Add the almonds, sesame seeds, plantain, three kinds of chile powders, cinnamon, salt, shredded tortillas, onion, garlic, and tomatoes to a blender or food processor. Process until pureed. Add a little of the chicken broth and continue to process to make a smooth paste.

In a large, heavy saucepan, stir together the paste and chicken broth, cooking over medium heat. Add the chocolate and stir until melted. Continue to cook until the sauce is thickened. Taste and adjust seasonings, if necessary.

Place the turkey breast in a roasting pan and insert a meat thermometer. Cover with the prepared sauce and bake, covered, until the internal temperature reaches 160 degrees F. Reserve any extra sauce to pass with the turkey. Any leftover sauce may be frozen. Remove the turkey from the oven and allow to sit for about 10 minutes before slicing.

*Sweet Dreams*
xxxxxx

## Chocolate Pear Cake

xxxxx

*Serves 10*

4 ripe pears, peeled, cored, and cut into 1-inch cubes

2 tablespoons butter

¼ cup brown sugar, firmly packed

½ teaspoon ground cinnamon

Butter for pan

¾ cup all-purpose flour

½ cup finely ground toasted almonds (see page 13)

¼ cup cocoa powder

½ teaspoon baking powder

½ teaspoon baking soda

½ teaspoon ground cinnamon

4 tablespoons butter, softened

¾ cup sugar

1 teaspoon vanilla extract

2 eggs

⅓ cup milk

1 cup Basic Chocolate Sauce (see page 15)

2 tablespoons pear liqueur, such as Poire William

*In an off-the-beaten-path village in Italy, there's a small trattoria where the proprietor makes an incredible chocolate cake studded with juicy chunks of pear. If you ask her for the recipe, she won't give it to you—because then, she says, you'll have no reason to return. This is only an approximation of her recipe, so guess where we'll be going on our next trip to Italy.*

Sauté the pears, butter, brown sugar, and cinnamon over medium heat until the pears are coated and tender, about 4 minutes. Set aside.

Preheat oven to 350 degrees F. Butter a 9-inch round baking pan, line the bottom with parchment, and then butter the parchment.

Sift together the flour, almonds, cocoa powder, baking powder, baking soda, and cinnamon. In a separate bowl, cream the softened 4 tablespoons of butter. Add the sugar and beat until fluffy. Add the vanilla and eggs, beating well. Gradually add the flour mixture, stirring well after each addition. Fold in the milk and pears. Spread the mixture in the prepared pan and bake until a cake tester comes out clean, approximately 55 minutes.

Remove from the oven and cool in the pan on a wire rack for 20 minutes. Invert the cake onto a serving plate and remove the parchment. Allow to cool completely. Just before serving, warm the chocolate sauce and stir in the pear liqueur. Pour over the cake, completely covering the top and allowing the sauce to run down the sides.

# Chocolate Piñon Cake

xxxxxx

*This cake takes hours and is expensive to make, but the end result is well worth it, especially for a special occasion. See Appendix I for tips on melting the chocolate.*

Preheat oven to 350 degrees F. Grease and flour the bottoms and sides of four 8 x 1½-inch round cake pans. Set aside.

For the cake batter: Separate 9 eggs. In a large mixing bowl, cream together the butter and sugar until fluffy, and then begin adding the 9 egg yolks, one at a time, beating well after each addition. Add the melted chocolate and then stir in the ground piñons, bread crumbs, and milk. Beat the 9 egg whites to stiff peaks, and then gently fold them into the batter, mixing until few streaks remain. Pour into the prepared pans. Bake for 15 minutes. Remove from the oven and cool on wire racks for about 10 minutes, then remove from the pans and cool for at least 1 hour. This step can be done a day ahead.

For the filling: In a heavy saucepan, combine the confectioners' sugar and cornstarch, and then gradually beat in the 4 egg yolks. Stir in the milk. Cook over medium heat, stirring constantly, until the mixture thickens to a custard consistency. Remove from heat, and add the liqueur and vanilla. Cool slightly, and then cover the surface with plastic wrap. In a glass bowl, melt the semisweet chocolate in the microwave until softened but not liquid (90 degrees F on a candy thermometer). Cream the softened butter with the melted chocolate and then gradually stir in the custard mixture. Cool and cover the surface with plastic wrap until the cake is ready to assemble.

*Serves 16*

9 eggs, separated

¾ cup butter, softened

⅔ cup sugar

5 ounces bittersweet chocolate, melted and slightly cooled

2 cups ground piñons

⅓ cup dry white bread crumbs

2 tablespoons milk

1 cup sifted confectioners' sugar

1 tablespoon cornstarch

4 beaten egg yolks

¼ cup milk

2 tablespoons hazelnut liqueur, such as Frangelico

1 teaspoon vanilla extract

3 ounces semisweet chocolate

½ cup butter, softened

1 ounce unsweetened chocolate

1 tablespoon butter

1 cup sifted confectioners' sugar

1 teaspoon vanilla extract

Hot water as needed

½ cup toasted piñons, for garnish  (see page 13)

For the glaze: Place the unsweetened chocolate and tablespoon of butter in a microwave-safe dish. Heat in the microwave on medium power for 30 seconds. Stir and heat in 10-second increments until melted. Add the confectioners' sugar and vanilla, stirring until smooth, and adding hot water, 1 tablespoon at a time, until the mixture reaches a pourable consistency.

To assemble: Place one layer of cake, top down, on a serving plate. Cover with ⅓ of the filling. Alternate layers of cake and filling, ending with a cake layer, top-side up. Pour the glaze over, allowing it to run down the sides of the layers. Sprinkle the top with toasted piñons.

Refrigerate until serving time.

# Chocolate-Orange Angel Food Shortcake

XXXXXX

*The chocolate flavor is understated and muted in the cake, but makes a nice complement to the orange.*

Place oven rack at the lowest position and preheat the oven to 325 degrees F.

Sift together 1 cup of the sugar with the flour, cocoa powder, and salt. In a medium-sized bowl, beat the egg whites at medium speed until foamy. Add the cream of tartar and orange liqueur and beat at high speed until soft peaks form. Continue beating and gradually add the remaining ½ cup of sugar and the orange zest. Beat until the peaks are firmer, but not stiff. Do not over-beat. Gently fold in the dry ingredients in ¼-cup increments until no streaks remain, taking care not to deflate the egg whites. Spread into an ungreased 10-inch tube pan and bake 50–60 minutes or until the cake is firm and springs back when touched. Remove from the oven, turn upside down, and cool on a rack.

While the cake is cooling, wash the strawberries, raspberries, and blackberries and place them in bowl. Add the mandarin oranges, orange liqueur, and sugar. Gently mix together. Allow to sit at room temperature for about 30 minutes before serving.

To serve, remove the cake from the pan and slice into 8 pieces. Place each on a serving plate and top with the fruit mixture. Add a dollop of whipped cream.

*Serves 8*

1½ cups sugar

1 cup flour

¼ cup cocoa powder

¼ teaspoon salt

12 egg whites at room temperature

1½ teaspoons cream of tartar

3 teaspoons orange liqueur, such as Grand Marnier

3 teaspoons grated orange zest

1 cup fresh strawberries

1 cup fresh raspberries

1 cup fresh blackberries

1 can mandarin orange slices, drained

¼ cup orange liqueur

¼ cup sugar

Whipped cream, for garnish

## Chocolate Tangerine Pound Cake with Tangerine Whipped Cream

XXXXXX

*Serves 8*

10 tablespoons butter, softened

1¾ cups brown sugar, firmly packed

2 eggs

1 teaspoon vanilla extract

2 cups sifted flour

1 teaspoon baking soda

½ cup cocoa powder

Pinch of salt

½ cup sour cream

¾ cup fresh tangerine juice

1 cup whipping cream, chilled

¼ cup confectioners' sugar

2 tablespoons grated tangerine zest

*A nice, light dessert with one of my favorite taste combinations: chocolate and tangerine.*

Preheat oven to 325 degrees F. Grease and flour a 9 x 5 x 3-inch loaf pan.

In a large bowl, beat the butter until creamy. Add the brown sugar, eggs, and vanilla, and beat until light and fluffy. In a separate bowl, sift together the flour, baking soda, cocoa powder, and salt. Add one-quarter of the flour mixture to the sugar mixture, stir, and then add one-third of the sour cream. Combine well. Repeat, alternating additions of flour and sour cream until the batter is smooth. Add the tangerine juice and stir until combined. Pour the batter into the prepared pan.

Bake 65–75 minutes or until a cake tester comes out clean. Cool the cake in the pan on a wire rack for 15 minutes. Remove from the pan and cool completely on the wire rack. Meanwhile, chill a metal bowl and beaters.

Pour the cold whipping cream into the chilled bowl and beat until soft peaks form. Add the confectioners' sugar and tangerine zest. Beat until stiff peaks form.

Slice the cake, place slices on dessert plates, and top each slice with a dollop of the whipped cream.

# Chocolate Cake with Raspberry Ganache

XXXXXX

*Serves 6*

2 cups all-purpose flour

2 cups sugar

2 teaspoons baking soda

½ cup cocoa powder

¼ teaspoon salt

1 cup canola oil

1 cup buttermilk

2 eggs, slightly beaten

1 teaspoon vanilla extract

1 cup boiling water

8 ounces bittersweet chocolate, finely chopped

¾ cup heavy cream

½ cup raspberry jam, melted

1 pint fresh raspberries, washed and dried, for garnish

Bittersweet chocolate curls for garnish

*This is a simple from-scratch cake, but if you're in a hurry, you can always use a mix. The ganache is so rich, no one will ever know.*

Preheat oven to 350 degrees F. Grease and flour two 9-inch cake pans.

Sift together the flour, sugar, baking soda, cocoa powder, and salt. Create a well in the center and pour in the oil, buttermilk, eggs, and vanilla. Stir together until combined. Add the boiling water and mix well. Pour the batter into the prepared pans and bake until a cake tester comes out clean, about 35 minutes. Remove from the oven and allow to cool on a rack in the pans for 15 minutes. Remove from the pans and allow to cool completely.

To make the ganache: Place the chopped chocolate in a bowl. In a medium saucepan over medium heat, bring the cream to a simmer, and melt the raspberry jam in another small saucepan. Pour the cream over the chocolate and allow to sit for 1 minute. Add the raspberry jam and stir until the chocolate is melted. Cool to a spreadable consistency.

To assemble, place 1 cake layer on a serving plate, bottom-side up. Spread with a thick layer of ganache. Place the remaining cake layer on top, right side up. Center over the bottom layer. Frost the top and sides with the remaining ganache. Pile berries in the center of the top layer, and cover with chocolate curls.

# Molten Chocolate Cakes

xxxxxx

*These rich chocolate cakes include a velvety surprise in the center. You can prepare them a day in advance, refrigerate, and then bake them right before serving.*

Butter 4 ramekins or custard cups and sugar the insides. Chill a small glass plate in the freezer.

For the centers: Melt the chocolate and butter together (see Appendix I). Remove 5 tablespoons of this mixture into a small bowl and add the liqueur, stirring until well blended. Keep the remaining chocolate warm over a water bath. Pour the liqueur–chocolate mixture onto the chilled plate and return to the freezer until it is firm, about 5 minutes. Remove from the freezer and scrape into four small balls. Refrigerate.

For the cake: Remove the warm chocolate from the water bath and whisk in the cocoa powder and 2 egg yolks. In a mixing bowl, beat the 3 egg whites and cream of tartar until soft. Beat in the sugar and continue beating until medium soft peaks form. Gently fold some of the egg whites into the chocolate mixture until combined. Fold in the remaining egg whites just until no streaks remain, taking care not to deflate the whites. Remove the chocolate balls from the refrigerator and place one in the center of each prepared ramekin. Spoon in the cake batter, dividing evenly among the dishes. If you plan to bake them later, seal each ramekin with plastic wrap and refrigerate.

To bake, preheat the oven to 400 degrees F. Remove the plastic wrap from the ramekins and place on a baking sheet. Bake for

*Serves 4*

**Butter, for preparing ramekins**

**Sugar, for preparing ramekins**

**6 ounces bittersweet chocolate, finely chopped**

**6 tablespoons unsalted butter, cut into pieces**

**3 tablespoons vanilla-flavored liqueur, such as Tuaca**

**2 tablespoons cocoa powder**

**2 eggs, separated**

**1 additional egg white**

**Pinch of cream of tartar**

**3 tablespoons sugar**

about 15 minutes until puffed, or until a cake tester comes out clean. Remove from oven and allow to cool for a few minutes before serving.

## Arroz con Leche y Chocolate (Chocolate Rice Pudding)

xxxxxx

*Serves 4*

1 cup uncooked rice

1 cinnamon stick

2 cups water

½ cup sugar

4 ounces premium bittersweet chocolate, melted and slightly cooled

3 eggs, separated

1 cup milk

*When using eggs raw, it's important to take care to prevent salmonella contamination. Make sure the eggs are fresh and the shells are clean and undamaged. To separate, rather than rocking the yolk back and forth between the shell halves, use one hand to crack the egg into your other hand over a bowl. Allow the whites to run between your fingers into the bowl, and then put the yolk into a separate bowl. This reduces the chance of the shell coming into contact with the egg.*

In a saucepan over high heat, bring the rice, cinnamon stick, and water to a boil. Reduce heat, cover, and cook until the rice is dry, about 30 minutes. Remove the cinnamon stick.

Beat together the sugar, melted chocolate, egg yolks, and milk until combined. Add to the rice and cook over medium heat, stirring constantly, until the mixture is thickened. Remove from heat. Beat the egg whites until stiff, and then gently fold in the rice mixture. Serve warm.

# Chocolate Zabaglione Crepes with Cherry Port Reduction

XXXXXX

*You can do most of this a day ahead of time, so it makes an easy brunch dish as well as a perfect end to dinner.*

The sauce: Bring the port to a boil in a large heavy saucepan. Add the cherries. Reduce the heat to a simmer and allow the mixture to cook down until thick and reduced, about 1½ hours. This can be done a day in advance and refrigerated.

The crepes: Combine the flour, water, milk, eggs, and unsalted butter in the bowl of a food processor. Pulse until well blended, about 20 seconds. Scrape down the sides and allow the batter to rest for about 1 hour.

Brush an 8-inch skillet or crepe pan with some of the additional melted butter, then heat over medium-high until the pan begins to smoke. Pour ¼ cup of batter into the pan, swirling to coat the bottom. Heat for about 45 seconds or until the bottom is browned, and then flip the crepe and cook the other side until lightly browned, about 10 seconds. Remove from the pan and allow it to cool on a flat surface. Continue in the same fashion until all of the batter is used, brushing the pan with melted butter between each crepe. You should have 18 crepes.

Crepes can be stored in a stack, separated with waxed paper, then wrapped in plastic and refrigerated. They may also be frozen for up to three months.

*Serves 6*

3 cups port wine

1 cup dried tart cherries

1 cup flour

½ cup water

¾ cup milk

2 large eggs

3 tablespoons unsalted butter, melted and cooled

2 tablespoons melted butter, for cooking crepes

¼ cup heavy cream

4 ounces bittersweet chocolate, finely chopped

8 large egg yolks

½ cup sugar

¼ cup dry Marsala

The chocolate zabaglione: Place the heavy cream in a heavy small saucepan and bring to a simmer over medium heat. Place the chopped chocolate in a glass bowl. Pour the heated cream over the chocolate. Allow to sit for 1 minute, and then stir until chocolate is melted and smooth. Set aside and keep warm.

Whisk the egg yolks, sugar, and Marsala in a round-bottomed zabaglione pan or the top of a double boiler until thickened and light yellow. Set this pan over a saucepan of simmering water without allowing the bottom of the pan to touch the water. Whisk the egg mixture briskly until it is thick and doubled in volume, about 5 minutes. Whisk and cook another 3 minutes. Remove from the heat.

Gently fold the melted chocolate mixture into the egg mixture until combined. Chill until serving time.

To assemble the crepes, place several spoonfuls of zabaglione down the center of each crepe, then roll. Place three crepes, seam-side down, on each dessert plate. Spoon cherry port reduction over the crepes.

# Chocolate Mint Panna Cotta
xxxxxx

*Panna cotta is a simple Italian dessert, but the addition of the mint makes it a complex, yet refreshing, end to a summer meal.*

Heat the half-and-half in a small saucepan until simmering, then add the mint leaves. Remove from heat and allow to steep, covered, for 1 hour. Strain to remove the leaves and return the half-and-half to a heavy saucepan.

Soften the gelatin in the cold water.

Add the heavy cream and sugar to the half-and-half and bring to a simmer, then add the softened gelatin and chopped chocolate. Stir constantly until the sugar, gelatin, and chocolate are melted. Pour into 8 glass ramekins and refrigerate until firm, about 2 hours.

To serve, puddle warm chocolate sauce on each of eight serving plates. Dip each ramekin into warm, not hot, water for about 10 seconds to loosen the pudding, then invert onto a prepared serving plate. Drizzle with a little more chocolate sauce and garnish with a mint leaf.

*Serves 8*

2 cups half-and-half

½ cup mint leaves, packed

1 package gelatin

⅓ cup cold water

2 cups heavy cream

¼ cup sugar

8 ounces bittersweet chocolate, finely chopped

Basic Chocolate Sauce, for garnish (see page 15)

8 mint leaves, for garnish

# Cream Puffs with Cinnamon Chocolate Whipped Cream

xxxxxx

*My mom is the cream puff queen—she makes them for special occasions at the office, and people clamor for them. She uses sweetened whipped cream for hers, but what can it hurt to add a little chocolate?*

Preheat the oven to 425 degrees F. Line a baking sheet with parchment paper.

Melt the butter in the water over medium heat and bring to a rapid boil. Add the flour all at once, raise the saucepan above the heat, and stir vigorously with a wooden spoon until the paste forms a smooth ball in the middle of the pan. Return to the heat and stir for 30 seconds. Remove the pan from the heat. Add 1 egg and beat until smooth and fluffy. Add the remaining eggs one at a time, beating until smooth and glossy after each addition. Drop the dough by heaping tablespoonfuls onto the baking sheet, about 2 inches apart.

Bake for 20 minutes, and then reduce the heat to 350 degrees F and bake for another 20 minutes. Remove from the oven and then transfer to a wire rack to cool completely. Meanwhile, chill a mixing bowl and beaters.

Pour the whipping cream into the chilled bowl and beat at high speed until it begins to hold its shape. Add the cinnamon and sugar and beat until stiff peaks form. Melt the chocolate (see Appendix I). Fold about ½ cup of whipped cream into the chocolate and stir until blended. Gently fold in the remaining whipped cream.

*Serves 8*

¼ cup butter

1 cup water

1 cup minus 1 tablespoon flour

4 eggs

2 cups heavy whipping cream

½ teaspoon ground cinnamon

¼ cup confectioners' sugar

4 ounces semisweet chocolate, chopped

Confectioners' sugar for garnish

To assemble, slice the cream puffs in half and remove any excess dough in the centers. Fill the bottoms with whipped cream, and then replace the tops. Sift confectioners' sugar over the top of each. Serve immediately.

## Chocolate Bread Pudding with Cinnamon Crème Anglaise

xxxxx

*Serves 8*

¼ cup unsalted butter

8 cups cubed cinnamon raisin bread

½ cup crushed walnuts

5 ounces bittersweet chocolate

2 cups whipping cream

1 cup whole milk

8 egg yolks

⅔ cup firmly packed brown sugar

1 teaspoon vanilla extract

2 cups whipping cream

½ cup milk

3 cinnamon sticks

6 egg yolks

½ cup sugar

1 teaspoon vanilla extract

*Gene Adcock is a sculptor, man-about-town, and raconteur. He's also a fabulous cook, well known for his Aspen-area parties such as the Croquet Ball. This is one of his favorite desserts, with a couple of minor modifications.*

In a heavy skillet over medium heat, melt the butter and then add the bread cubes and walnuts, stirring until the bread is toasted. Set aside.

Place the bittersweet chocolate in the bowl of a food processor. Combine the 2 cups of cream and 1 cup of milk in a heavy medium saucepan. Over medium heat, bring just to a boil, and then remove from heat. Pulse the food processor to chop the chocolate and then, with the machine running, slowly pour the heated cream mixture into the processor. Process until the chocolate is melted.

In a large bowl, whisk together the 8 egg yolks, brown sugar, and vanilla until well blended. Slowly add the chocolate cream to the egg yolk mixture, whisking constantly. Place the bread cubes in another large bowl and pour the chocolate mixture over the top. Allow to stand for about 1 hour, or until the bread absorbs the liquid, stirring gently every 10 minutes or so to keep all of the bread coated.

Preheat oven to 325 degrees F. Divide the bread mixture evenly between two 8 x 4 x 2-inch loaf pans. Cover each one with foil and poke several small holes in the foil to allow steam to escape. Place the pans in a large roasting pan and add enough hot water to the roasting pan to reach one inch up the sides of the loaf pans. Place in the oven and bake for 1½ hours, or until the pudding is set and a toothpick inserted in the center comes out clean.

Remove from the oven, remove the pans from the water bath, and place the pans on a rack to cool for 30 minutes.

To make the custard sauce, bring the 2 cups of cream, ½ cup of milk, and the cinnamon sticks to a boil, then remove from heat, cover, and allow to sit for about 1 hour. Strain the cinnamon sticks out of the cream mixture and return the mixture to medium heat. In a medium bowl, whisk together the 6 egg yolks, sugar, and vanilla, and then slowly whisk it into the cream mixture. Stir constantly until the mixture thickens and comes to a boil. Remove from heat and allow to cool.

To serve, place a serving of the bread pudding into a dessert dish and ladle custard sauce over the top.

## Earl Grey Chocolate Mousse

xxxxxx

*Serves 4*

1½ cups whipping cream

4 Earl Grey teabags

13 ounces premium
bittersweet chocolate

2 tablespoons butter

2 large egg yolks,
slightly beaten

2 tablespoons sugar

1 teaspoon vanilla extract

Chocolate shavings,
for garnish

*Earl Grey gets its distinctive flavor from bergamot, a variety of sour orange. Use a high-quality, fresh tea, and don't let it steep any longer than 5 minutes or it will become bitter.*

In a medium saucepan, bring the whipping cream to a simmer over medium heat. Remove from heat and add the teabags. Allow to steep for 5 minutes. Remove the teabags and refrigerate the cream until well chilled (at least 1 hour).

Finely chop the chocolate, and then melt the chocolate and butter together (see Appendix I). Cool slightly and whisk in the egg yolks. Cool to room temperature.

Chill a mixing bowl and beaters. Pour the chilled whipping cream into the bowl and beat until soft peaks form, then add the sugar and vanilla and beat until stiff peaks form. Gently fold the cooled chocolate into the cream. Spoon into serving dishes and garnish with chocolate shavings.

## Chocolate Natillas

xxxxxx

*Serves 8*

3½ cups half-and-half

8 ounces premium bittersweet chocolate, finely chopped

4 eggs

¼ cup granulated sugar

½ teaspoon ground cinnamon

1 teaspoon vanilla extract

3 tablespoons confectioners' sugar

Ground cinnamon, for garnish

*This simple custard can be prepared with or without the meringues, but they make an interesting presentation.*

In a large saucepan over medium heat, bring the half-and-half to a simmer. Add the chopped chocolate and stir until melted. Remove from heat.

Separate two eggs, reserving the whites. Beat together the 2 egg yolks with the 2 remaining whole eggs. Add granulated sugar and cinnamon, beating until fluffy. Pour about ¼ cup of the melted chocolate mixture into the eggs, whisking constantly. Whisk the egg mixture into the melted chocolate mixture remaining in the pan and cook over medium heat, stirring constantly, until the mixture thickens and begins to boil. Remove from heat, stir in vanilla, and pour into custard cups or ramekins. Cover the surface of each with plastic wrap and chill.

Beat the remaining egg whites until thickened. Add the confectioners' sugar and beat until medium soft peaks form. In a large skillet, heat about two inches of water to a simmer. Drop the beaten egg whites by the tablespoon on to the surface of the simmering water. Cover and let steam until firm. Using a slotted spoon, remove the meringues from the water and place on a rack to cool. Just before serving, top each ramekin of custard with a meringue and sprinkle with cinnamon.

## Heavenly Trifle

xxxxxx

*This is my family's favorite Christmas dessert. Serve it in a glass bowl to show off the layers.*

For the cake: Preheat the oven to 350 degrees F. Grease and flour an 8 x 8-inch baking pan.

In a small mixing bowl, stir together the flour, sugar, cocoa powder, baking soda, and salt. Make a well in the center and add the egg, canola oil, water, and vanilla. Stir to combine, and then beat at medium speed for 2 minutes. Pour into the prepared pan and bake for 35 minutes. Remove from the oven and allow to cool on a wire rack for about 10 minutes. Remove the cake from the pan and allow to cool completely.

For the filling: In a heavy saucepan, combine the milk, cream, sugar, cornstarch, and salt. Bring to a simmer and cook, whisking constantly, until the sugar is dissolved and the mixture thickens, 3–4 minutes. Remove from heat.

In a medium bowl, beat the egg yolks until thick and light yellow, about 3 minutes. Slowly add about ½ cup of the hot milk mixture to the egg yolks, whisking constantly. Stir the egg mixture into the pan of the hot milk mixture and return to heat. Cook over medium-low heat, stirring constantly for 1 minute. Bring to a simmer, stirring constantly with a wooden spoon, and cook until thickened, about 2 minutes. Remove from heat and stir in the butter, vanilla, and sherry. Allow to cool.

*(continued)*

*Serves 10*

**1⅔ cups flour**

**1 cup sugar**

**3 tablespoons cocoa powder**

**½ teaspoon baking soda**

**½ teaspoon salt**

**1 egg**

**⅓ cup canola oil**

**¾ cup water**

**½ teaspoon vanilla extract**

**1¾ cups milk**

**1 cup heavy cream**

**¾ cup sugar**

**3 tablespoons cornstarch**

**⅛ teaspoon salt**

**3 egg yolks**

**1 tablespoon unsalted butter, cut into pieces**

**2 teaspoons vanilla extract**

**¼ cup sweet sherry**

**¾ cup apricot preserves**

**1 cup heavy cream**

**1 tablespoon confectioners' sugar**

**½ teaspoon vanilla extract**

**½ cup slivered almonds, for garnish**

To assemble the trifle, slice the cake in half horizontally and spread the bottom half with apricot preserves. Replace the top half and cut the cake into 1-inch cubes. Place a small amount of the pudding in the bottom of a trifle bowl or other clear glass 2½-quart bowl. Add a layer of cake cubes, then a layer of pudding. Repeat until the bowl is full. Cover with plastic wrap and refrigerate until just before serving.

To serve, chill a mixing bowl and beaters. Pour the cream into the bowl and beat until soft peaks form. Add the sugar and vanilla and continue to beat until the peaks are semi-stiff. Spread the whipped cream in a thick layer over the trifle and sprinkle with slivered almonds.

## Coconut Pecan Bonbons

xxxxxx

*I make these every Christmas, and the only problem with them is that they make you want to do nothing but sit on the couch and eat bonbons. If you don't want to take the time to temper the chocolate, you can add a chunk of paraffin to the melting dipping chocolate, but for the best taste, texture, and appearance, it's best to temper.*

In a large mixing bowl, combine the sugar, butter, condensed milk, coconut, and pecans. Using your hands, mix until all ingredients are well combined. This can't be done with a mixer or a spoon, as the dough will be quite stiff. Cover the bowl with plastic wrap and chill for several hours or overnight.

Remove from the refrigerator, and after liberally dusting your hands with confectioners' sugar, roll the dough into 1-inch balls. Place on baking sheets, cover with plastic, and return to the refrigerator. Chill for 3 hours.

To "enrobe" the candies, melt and temper the chocolate (see Appendix I). Keep the chocolate over a pan of warm water to maintain the correct temperature. Using a dipping fork (see Appendix II), dunk each candy into the chocolate, remove, and place on waxed paper to harden. Alternatively, place a spoonful of chocolate in the palm of your hand and roll the candy in it to coat, then place on the waxed paper. When the chocolate has set, place in an airtight container and store in the refrigerator. Bring to room temperature before serving.

*Makes about 8 dozen*

1½ pounds confectioners' sugar, plus more for rolling bonbons

½ cup butter, at room temperature

1 can (14 ounces) sweetened condensed milk

1½ cups shredded coconut

4 cups finely chopped pecans

18 ounces bittersweet chocolate, finely chopped

## Holy Habanero Fudge

xxxxxx

*Makes about 64 pieces*

Butter for foiled pan

2¾ cups sugar

4 ounces premium
unsweetened chocolate,
chopped

1 teaspoon
habanero powder

3 tablespoons butter

1 cup half-and-half

1 tablespoon corn syrup

1 tablespoon vanilla extract

1 cup toasted piñons,
coarsely chopped
(see page 13)

*As the Mayans discovered, chile and chocolate work well together. The sugar and cream in the fudge cool down the heat of the habaneros, but if you think it might be too spicy for your taste, substitute a milder chile powder. Fudge can be tricky to make—you have to make sure the temperature gets high enough, and when you're stirring, don't scrape down the sides of the pan. Also, once you put the thermometer in, don't stir until you add the vanilla and nuts. The utensils have to be spotlessly clean. Practice makes perfect!*

Line an 8 x 8-inch baking pan with foil, and then butter the foil.

In a heavy saucepan, combine the sugar, chocolate, habanero powder, butter, half-and-half, and corn syrup. Bring to a boil over medium heat, stirring constantly. Avoid scraping down the sides of the pan, as this could cause the mixture to granulate. When the mixture comes to a boil, clip a candy thermometer to the pan and cook without stirring until the mixture reaches 234 degrees F (soft ball stage). Remove from heat and quickly stir in the vanilla and nuts. It's important to work fast as the mixture will begin to set up. Pour into the prepared pan and allow to cool at room temperature. When the fudge has cooled completely, turn it out of the pan onto a flat surface, peel away the foil, and cut into 1-inch squares. Store in a tightly sealed container.

## Almond Toffee

xxxxxx

*You might be tempted to stir when you add the ingredients to the pan and start cooking, but don't! Stirring can cause the sugar to crystallize, and nobody likes grainy toffee.*

Butter the bottom of a jelly roll pan.

Attach a candy thermometer to a heavy saucepan. Add the sugar, water, and corn syrup to the saucepan without stirring. Over medium heat, bring to a boil. Add the butter without stirring and allow to cook to 300 degrees F on the candy thermometer. Don't stir, as you don't want the sugar to crystallize on the sides of the pan.

When the mixture reaches the correct temperature and is darkened, pour it into the prepared pan. Allow to cool for 1 minute, and then sprinkle the chopped chocolate over the top. Use a spatula to smooth it as it melts. Sprinkle the top with almonds and allow to cool at room temperature for several hours, until set.

Use a heavy metal spatula to remove the candy from the pan and break into pieces. Store at a cool room temperature or refrigerate.

*Makes about 1 pound*

Butter for pan

1 cup sugar

¼ cup water

1 tablespoon light corn syrup

1 cup unsalted butter, cut into pieces

12 ounces premium bittersweet chocolate, finely chopped

½ cup toasted almonds, finely chopped (see page 13)

## Truffles

xxxxxx

*Makes about 10 dozen*

**1 recipe Basic Ganache (see page 15)**

**1 cup cocoa powder, Dutch process**

**1 cup toasted pecans, finely chopped**

**1 cup toasted macadamia nuts, finely chopped**

**1 cup shredded coconut, toasted**

**18 ounces premium bittersweet chocolate, finely chopped**

*Here is an easy and fun project to share with the kids or with friends. This is a basic recipe, but you can experiment with flavors and garnishes to show your culinary creativity. The prepared ganache should be covered with plastic wrap and allowed to sit at room temperature for several hours until set. This can be done a day ahead. See page 13 for tips on toasting the nuts; you can apply these tips to toasting coconut as well.*

Use a teaspoon to scoop out chunks of the prepared ganache. Place them on a baking sheet covered with wax paper or parchment. Place in the refrigerator until thoroughly chilled, about 2 hours.

To roll the truffles, chill your clean hands in ice water, then place one chilled scoop of ganache between your palms. Quickly squeeze into shape and roll into a ball. Place back on the baking sheet and refrigerate again for about 30 minutes.

While the truffle centers are chilling, line your work surface with wax paper or parchment. Place the cocoa powder, pecans, macadamia nuts, and coconut in small mounds on the paper.

Melt and temper the chocolate (see Appendix I). Keep the chocolate over a pan of hot water to maintain temperature, and use a dipping fork to dip the truffle centers one at a time into the chocolate. Allow excess chocolate to drip back into the pan, and then roll the enrobed truffle into the chosen garnish (cocoa powder, pecans, macadamia nuts, coconut, or a combination of the four). Place on the paper to set up. Alternatively, place a small amount of chocolate into the palm of one hand and with the other hand, roll the truffle center in the chocolate until coated, and then roll in the chosen garnish. Place on the paper to set up.

Continue dipping and rolling until all of the centers are enrobed and garnished. Store in an airtight container at a cool room temperature for up to 2 weeks.

## Chocolate Cherries Jubilee

xxxxxx

*It's a flashy presentation and a delicious combination.*

*Serves 4*

Scoop the ice cream into 4 dessert dishes. Top with the chocolate sauce. Melt the preserves in a small pan over medium heat, stirring frequently. Stir in the cinnamon. Add Cognac and heat gently without stirring. Using a long match, ignite and spoon over the ice cream. Because the Cognac sits on top of the cherry sauce, it will burn with a gentle blue flame and then gradually extinguish itself. Just remember to keep flammables away while it's still burning.

1 pint premium cherry chocolate ice cream, such as Ben & Jerry's Cherry Garcia

½ cup Basic Chocolate Sauce, at room temperature (see page 15)

½ cup cherry preserves

Pinch of ground cinnamon

3 tablespoons Cognac

## Profiteroles

xxxxxx

*Serves 8*

¼ **cup butter**

1 **cup water**

1 **cup minus 1 tablespoon flour**

4 **eggs**

1 **cup Basic Chocolate Sauce (see page 15)**

1 **pint premium chocolate ice cream**

1 **pint premium coffee ice cream**

1 **pint premium vanilla bean ice cream**

*Here is an easy yet impressive dessert. If you want to get creative, use fruit sorbets in place of the ice cream and add raspberry flavoring to the sauce, or try mint ice cream with a mint-flavored sauce. Your only limits are your imagination and your taste buds.*

Preheat the oven to 425 degrees F. Line a baking sheet with parchment paper.

Melt the butter in the water over medium heat and bring to a rapid boil. Add the flour all at once, raise the saucepan above the heat, and stir vigorously with a wooden spoon until the paste forms a smooth ball in the middle of the pan. Return to the heat and stir for 30 seconds. Remove the pan from the heat. Add 1 egg and beat until smooth and fluffy. Add the remaining eggs one at a time, beating until smooth and glossy after each. Drop the dough by heaping teaspoons onto the baking sheet, about 2 inches apart, to yield 24 pastries.

Bake for 20 minutes, and then reduce the heat to 350 degrees F and bake for another 20 minutes. Remove from the oven and then transfer to a wire rack to cool completely.

To serve, split the puffs in half horizontally and remove any dough remaining in the centers. On each of 8 dessert plates, puddle 2 tablespoons of warm chocolate sauce. Place three puff-bottoms on each plate, and fill each with a different flavor of ice cream. Replace the tops, and then drizzle with the remaining chocolate sauce. Serve immediately.

# Adobe Mud Pie

xxxxxx

*My kids usually request this tasty treat instead of a birthday cake.*

*Serves 24*

Butter a 9 x 13-inch baking pan. Combine the crushed cookies and melted butter, then press into the bottom of the pan. Chill until firm.

Soften the ice cream to a spreadable consistency. Spread evenly over the cookie crust and place in freezer until solid.

Melt the chocolate and butter (see Appendix I). Add the sugar and milk to a medium heavy saucepan and bring to a boil, stirring constantly. Add the melted chocolate mixture and continue to stir until thickened. Remove from heat and add the vanilla. Cool to room temperature.

Remove the ice cream pan from the freezer and spread the cooled chocolate sauce over the top. Freeze again until solid.

Chill a mixing bowl and beaters. Add the cold cream to the bowl and beat at high speed until soft peaks form. Add the sugar and coffee liqueur, and then beat until the peaks are stiff. Spread over the chocolate layer and sprinkle with chocolate chips. Freeze again until firm.

To serve, remove from freezer and allow to soften slightly, about 10 minutes. Dip a knife in hot water and cut into pieces. Use warm spatula to remove the pieces from the pan.

30 chocolate sandwich cookies (such as Oreos), crushed

½ cup butter, melted

½ gallon coffee ice cream

4 ounces unsweetened chocolate

2 tablespoons butter

1 cup sugar

1 can evaporated milk

1 teaspoon vanilla extract

2 cups heavy cream

¼ cup confectioners' sugar

¼ cup coffee liqueur, such as Kahlúa

¾ cup semisweet chocolate chips

## Helado Azteca (Chocolate–Chile Ice Cream)

xxxxxx

*Makes 1½ quarts*

2 cups heavy cream

1 cup whole milk

6 egg yolks

⅓ cup dark brown sugar, firmly packed

1 teaspoon pure red chile powder

2 ounces unsweetened chocolate, chopped

6 ounces premium bittersweet chocolate, chopped

2 teaspoons ground cinnamon

2 tablespoons coffee liqueur, such as Kahlúa

*First, you experience the sensation of cold, and then the rich taste of chocolate floods your mouth. Finally, you get a nice warm tingle. It's a wonderful experience in contrasts.*

In a heavy saucepan, combine the cream and milk. Bring to a simmer. Beat together the egg yolks, brown sugar, and chile powder until fluffy. Pour about ½ cup of the hot milk into the egg yolk mixture, whisking constantly. Add the egg yolk mixture to the hot milk and cook over low heat, stirring constantly until the temperature reaches 170 degrees F on a candy thermometer. Remove from heat.

Melt the unsweetened and bittersweet chocolates (see Appendix I). Strain the custard mixture into the melted chocolate and stir until combined. Stir in the cinnamon and coffee liqueur. Allow to cool, and then freeze according to your ice-cream maker instructions.

# Frozen Chocolate Orange Mousse

XXXXXX

*A great summertime dessert for dinner on the patio.*

*Serves 6*

In a small saucepan, over medium heat, warm ½ cup of the cream with the espresso powder and sugar until the sugar is melted and the cream comes to a simmer. Meanwhile, place the chocolate in the bowl of a food processor and pulse to chop. When the cream comes to a simmer, pour it into the food processor, with the blade running, until the chocolate is smooth and melted. Set aside.

Beat the eggs and egg yolks until thickened and yellow, about 2 minutes. Beat in the remaining cup of cream and the melted chocolate mixture until well blended. Add the vanilla and orange liqueur, stirring to combine. Pour into 6 ramekins and place in the freezer until set, about 8 hours or overnight. Let sit at room temperature for a few minutes before serving. Garnish each ramekin with a dollop of whipped cream and a sprinkling of orange zest.

**1½ cups heavy cream**

**2 tablespoons espresso powder**

**¼ cup sugar**

**8 ounces premium bittersweet chocolate**

**2 eggs**

**2 egg yolks**

**½ teaspoon vanilla extract**

**¼ cup orange liqueur, such as Grand Marnier**

**Whipped cream, for garnish**

**Zest of 1 orange, for garnish**

# *Daring Drinks*

xxxxxx

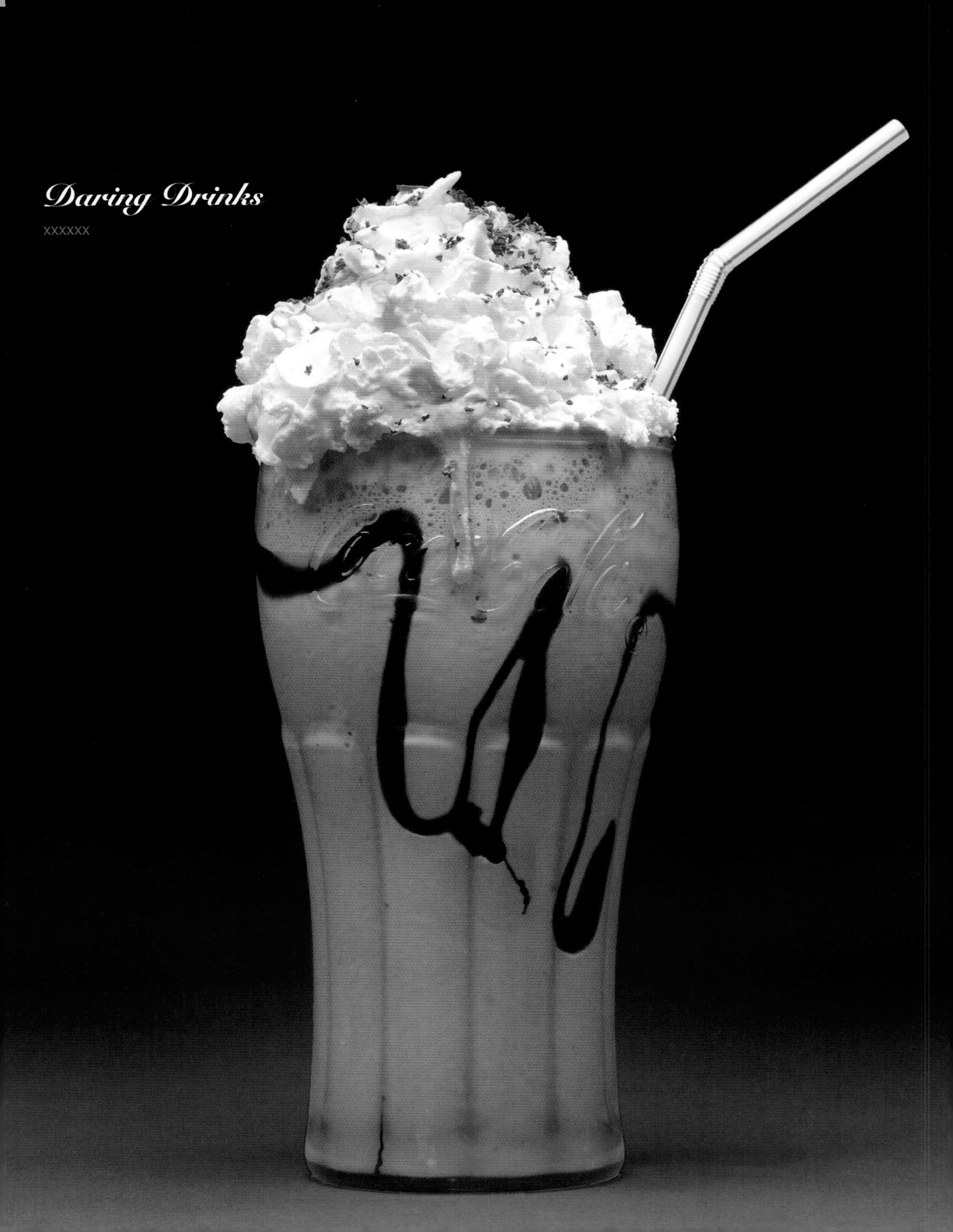

## Super Chocolaty Chocolate Shake

xxxxxx

*This is the creation of Tiana Carollo, the resident teenager in our house. She takes after her dad when it comes to being a chocolate lover. If a little chocolate is good, more is even better.*

Place the ice cream and chocolate milk in a blender, processing until well-mixed and smooth. Add the chocolate sauce and marshmallows. Pulse a few times to incorporate. Pour into a tall glass and top with whipped cream and chocolate sprinkles.

*Serves 1*

1 cup chocolate ice cream

¼ cup chocolate milk

3 tablespoons Basic Chocolate Sauce (see page 15, or use bottled hot fudge sauce)

¼ cup miniature marshmallows

Whipped cream, for garnish

Chocolate sprinkles, for garnish

## Caramel Mocha Shake (pictured)

xxxxxx

*You've just been out for a long run or a bike ride. You've burned off lots of calories. You deserve this rich and creamy reward.*

Place the espresso, milk, chocolate syrup, caramel syrup, and ice cream in a blender, processing until smooth. Pour into a tall glass and garnish with whipped cream and shaved chocolate.

*Serves 1*

1 shot espresso, cooled to room temperature

¼ cup milk

2 tablespoons Basic Chocolate Syrup (see page 16)

2 tablespoons caramel syrup

1 cup premium vanilla ice cream

Whipped cream, for garnish

Shaved bittersweet chocolate, for garnish

## Champurrado

xxxxxx

*Serves 6*

1½ cups masa harina
(corn flour, available in
Mexican groceries)

1 cup cold water

4 cups water

2 tablets Mexican chocolate

1 teaspoon salt

1½ cups sugar

1 teaspoon chile powder

*This breakfast drink is a Mexican tradition, and it's about as close as we can get to the early Spaniards' version of chocolate, made from three important New World ingredients.*

Stir together the masa harina and 1 cup of cold water until moistened. Bring 4 cups of water to a boil over high heat. Add the chocolate, salt, sugar, and chile powder. Once the chocolate is melted, stir in the masa harina mixture. Reduce the heat to medium and cook, stirring occasionally, for 10 minutes. Use an immersion blender or wire whisk to create froth on the top. Serve hot in mugs.

## Traditional Mexican Hot Chocolate

xxxxxx

*Serves 4*

4 cups milk

1 tablet Mexican
chocolate, grated

2 teaspoons vanilla extract

4 cinnamon sticks

*They say the happier the cook, the frothier the chocolate. If you want to be a real traditionalist, use a* molinillo *to add the froth.*

In a heavy saucepan, heat the milk. Add the grated chocolate, stirring occasionally until melted. Remove from heat, add the vanilla, and then, using an immersion blender or wire whisk, whip the hot chocolate until frothy. Pour into mugs and add cinnamon stick stirrers.

## On-the-Go Cocoa Mix

xxxxxx

*If you like to camp or backpack, here is the perfect mix to take along for those nights around the campfire. For breakfast, add coffee to make a tasty mocha.*

Mix together the powdered milk, cocoa powder, and sugar. Store in a large zippered storage bag. To serve, place ¼ cup of the mix in the bottom of a mug. Add a small amount of boiling water and stir to make a paste. Fill the mug with hot water, hot milk, or hot coffee and stir until blended.

*Makes 20 servings*

**4 cups instant non-fat powdered milk**

**½ cup cocoa powder**

**½ cup sugar**

## Almond Joy Hot Chocolate

xxxxxx

*This after-dinner drink doubles as dessert. Serve with a plate of amaretti for dipping in the hot chocolate.*

Heat the milk until simmering, add the chocolate, and stir until melted. Remove from heat, pour into 4 mugs, and add a shot of amaretto to each. Stir, and then top with a dollop of whipped cream and the crushed cookies.

*Serves 4*

**4 cups milk**

**8 ounces premium bittersweet chocolate, finely chopped**

**4 shots amaretto**

**Whipped cream, for garnish**

**4 crushed amaretti cookies (almond macaroons), for garnish**

## Mocha Buzz

xxxxxx

*Serves 2*

*A great drink for brunch on a cold winter morning.*

¾ cup milk

¾ cup half-and-half

4 ounces premium bittersweet chocolate, finely chopped

2 shots espresso

2 shots coffee liqueur, such as Kahlúa

In a saucepan, heat the milk and half-and-half just to a simmer. Add the chocolate and stir to melt. Remove from heat and stir in the espresso and Kahlúa. Pour into mugs.

## Orange Mocha

xxxxxx

*Serves 2*

*For a more pronounced orange flavor, you could add an orange liqueur to the mug before adding the hot chocolate.*

2 cups milk

4 strips orange peel, ½ inch by 2 inches

4 ounces bittersweet chocolate, finely chopped

2 shots espresso

Pinches of ground nutmeg, for garnish

In a heavy saucepan, heat the milk over medium heat until it begins to simmer. Add 2 of the strips of orange peel and allow to steep for 2 minutes. Remove the peel and add the chopped chocolate, stirring until melted. Stir in the espresso, pour into 2 mugs, and garnish with the remaining orange peel and a pinch of nutmeg.

# Captain Jack's Hot Chocolate

XXXXXX

*Yo ho ho, this one's not for the kids.*

*Serves 4*

In a heavy saucepan, stir together the cocoa powder, sugar, and water. Bring to a boil over medium-high heat, stirring constantly. Boil for 2 minutes, reduce heat, and add the milk. Heat through. Remove from heat and add the vanilla. Pour 1 shot of rum into each of 4 mugs, and then top with hot chocolate. Sprinkle each with a pinch of cinnamon.

¼ cup cocoa powder

½ cup sugar

⅓ cup water

4 cups milk

1 teaspoon vanilla extract

4 shots spiced rum

Pinches of ground cinnamon

*Storage* Like fine wine, chocolate will keep for a long time if it's stored properly. Because it picks up the odors of the food around it, you should place wrapped chocolate in airtight plastic bags and keep it away from things like onions, garlic, or other pungent foods in the pantry. Keep it in a dry, cool place—under 70 degrees F, if possible. If you keep it in the refrigerator, wrap it tightly in plastic and bring it to room temperature before use. If you live in a humid climate, unwrap the chocolate when you remove it from the refrigerator and then rewrap it in paper towels to absorb any condensation, which will affect the structure of the chocolate. You should never store chocolate in the freezer—freezing destroys the texture.

Sometimes you may notice that the surface has turned gray and looks powdery. This is "fat bloom," caused by fat cells crystallizing on the surface. Sugar bloom is caused by condensation, which melts and reforms the sugar crystals, also causing a gray coating on the surface. Both are a result of poor storage. Neither affects the flavor of the chocolate, although if you're nibbling it instead of cooking with it, the texture can be less than desirable.

*Melting* The ideal temperature for melting chocolate is between 104 and 113 degrees F. Because chocolate is easy to scorch, you should never melt it directly over the burner. Instead, use a hot water bath, which is even preferable to a double boiler. Chop the chocolate into small pieces and place in a glass bowl. Set the bowl into a pan of warm (but not simmering) water. Stir occasionally until the chocolate is melted. Water and chocolate don't mix, so take care not to drip or splash water into the melting chocolate, and make sure your stirring utensils are dry. Even a little moisture can cause the chocolate to seize up into an unworkable mass.

You can also use a microwave. Place the chocolate in a glass bowl (no need to cover it) and heat it on a medium power setting for 1 minute. Stir, and then heat again in 10-second increments, stirring between each, until the chocolate is melted.

*Tempering* If you're making chocolate decorations or truffles that require a smooth, glossy surface, the chocolate must be "tempered" after melting. Melting separates the fat molecules in the cocoa butter, and they become unstable. If you allow melted chocolate to harden without tempering, the cocoa butter rises to the top, and the finished product will be covered in fat bloom. Tempering allows the fat to recrystallize and protects the texture of the cooled chocolate.

While traditional methods of tempering can be messy and time-consuming, not to mention tricky, the easiest way is to use a microwave, rubber spatula, and instant-read thermometer. Place two-thirds of the finely chopped chocolate into a glass bowl and microwave on medium power for 30 seconds. Stir and check the temperature. Repeat until the chocolate reaches a temperature of between 100 and 110 degrees F. Remove from the microwave and begin adding the final third of the chocolate in small amounts, stirring until each addition melts. The chocolate should cool to a temperature of between 87 and 91 degrees F, which is the temperature for working. Keep it over a hot water bath while you're working with it, to maintain the proper temperature.

Gourmet groceries and even many mainstream grocery stores carry a wide variety of chocolate, but if you want to explore, visit some of the many Internet resources. You'll find chocolates from around the world and all of the equipment necessary to create your own chocolate specialties. Below are just a few of the better known.

## APPENDIX II: CHOCOLATE AND CHILE POWDER RESOURCES

### For chocolate:

WWW.CHOCOLATESOURCE.COM  Gourmet chocolates from around the world for both fine eating and baking.

WWW.LEPICERIE.COM  Gourmet chocolate and other food products, along with kitchenware.

WWW.CHEFSCATALOG.COM  Chocolate for baking, along with kitchenware and supplies.

WWW.WORLDWIDECHOCOLATE.COM  A huge selection of gourmet and specialty chocolates from around the world, including organics and chocolate tasting kits.

WWW.PASTRYCHEF.COM  Everything you would ever need to become a pastry chef, including enrobing bowls, dipping forks, chocolate chippers, and shavers.

### For chile powders:

WWW.SANTAFESCHOOLOFCOOKING.COM  Offers a selection of everything chile, including dried chiles, chile powders, and chipotles in adobo.

WWW.HOTCHILE.COM  *The* source for chiles and powders from Hatch, New Mexico.

**INDEX**

Adobe Mud Pie, 65
Almond Joy Hot Chocolate, 71
Almond Toffee, 61
ancho chile powder
 Turkey Mole, 36
Arroz con Leche y Chocolate, 46
Basic Chocolate Sauce, 15
Basic Chocolate Syrup, 16
Basic Ganache, 15
beverages
 Almond Joy Hot Chocolate, 71
 Captain Jack's Hot Chocolate, 73
 Caramel Mocha Shake, 69
 Champurrado, 70
 Mocha Buzz, 72
 On-the-Go Cocoa Mix, 71
 Orange Mocha, 72
 Super Chocolaty Chocolate
 Shake, 69
 Traditional Mexican Hot
 Chocolate, 70
Biscochitos, Chocolate Piñon, 30
bittersweet chocolate, 11
 Almond Joy Hot Chocolate, 71
 Almond Toffee, 61
 Arroz con Leche y Chocolate
 (Chocolate Rice Pudding), 46
 Basic Chocolate Sauce, 15
 Basic Ganache, 15
 Chocolate Bread Pudding with
 Cinnamon Crème Anglaise, 52
 Chocolate Cake with Raspberry
 Ganache, 44
 Chocolate Mint Panna Cotta, 49
 Chocolate Natillas, 56
 Chocolate Piñon Cake, 39
 Chocolate Stuffed French Toast
 with Orange Marmalade Sauce,
 22
 Chocolate Zabaglione Crepes
 with Cherry Port Reduction, 47
 Coconut Pecan Bonbons, 59
 Double Chocolate Cherry
 Muffins, 23
 Earl Grey Chocolate Mousse, 54
 Frozen Chocolate Orange

 Mousse, 67
 Grilled Chocolate–Peanut-Butter
 Sandwiches, 26
 Helado Azteca (Chocolate–Chile
 Ice Cream), 66
 Marbled Double Chocolate Chip
 Cookies, 28
 Mocha Buzz, 72
 Molten Chocolate Cakes, 45
 Orange Mocha, 72
 Truffles, 62
Bonbons, Coconut Pecan, 59
breakfast dishes
 Chocolate Chip Pecan pancakes,
 18
 Chocolate Stuffed French Toast
 with Orange Marmalade Sauce,
 22
 Double Chocolate Cherry
 Muffins, 23
 Gianduia Puff Pastry, 21
Brownies, Espresso, 31
cakes
 Chocolate Cake with Raspberry
 Ganache, 44
 Chocolate-Orange Angel Food
 Shortcake, 41
 Chocolate Pear Cake, 38
 Chocolate Piñon Cake, 39
 Chocolate Tangerine Pound Cake
 with Tangerine Whipped Cream,
 42
 Molten Chocolate Cakes, 45
Captain Jack's Hot Chocolate, 73
Caramel Mocha Shake, 69
Champurrado, 70
Chicken, Pecan Chile, 33
chile powders, 13, 77
Chile-Rubbed Steaks, 35
Chili, Smokin' Hot, 34
chipotle chile powder
 Smokin' Hot Chili, 34
 Turkey Mole, 36
Chocolate Bread Pudding with
 Cinnamon Crème Anglaise, 52
Chocolate Burritos, 25

Chocolate Cake with Raspberry Ganache, 44
Chocolate Cherries Jubilee, 63
Chocolate Chile Ice Cream, 66
Chocolate Chip Pecan Pancakes, 18
Chocolate Mint Panna Cotta, 49
Chocolate Natillas, 56
Chocolate-Orange Angel Food Shortcake, 41
Chocolate Pear Cake, 38
Chocolate Piñon Biscochitos, 30
Chocolate Piñon Cake, 39
Chocolate Pizza, 25
Chocolate Pumpkin Empanadas, 27
Chocolate Rice Pudding, 46
Chocolate Stuffed French Toast with Orange Marmalade Sauce, 22
Chocolate Tangerine Pound Cake with Tangerine Whipped Cream, 42
Chocolate Zabaglione Crepes with Cherry Port Reduction, 47
Cocoa Mix, On-the-Go, 71
Coconut Pecan Bonbons, 59
Cookies, Marbled Double Chocolate Chip, 28
Cream Puffs with Cinnamon Chocolate Whipped Cream, 51
Crepes, Chocolate Zabaglione, with Cherry Port Reduction, 47
dark chocolate (*see bittersweet chocolate*)
desserts (*see also cakes; frozen dishes*)
    Almond Toffee, 61
    Arroz con Leche y Chocolate, 46
    Chocolate Bread Pudding with Cinnamon Crème Anglaise, 52
    Chocolate Mint Panna Cotta, 49
    Chocolate Natillas, 56
    Chocolate Piñon Biscochitos, 30
    Chocolate Pumpkin Empanadas, 27
    Chocolate Rice Pudding, 46
    Chocolate Zabaglione Crepes with Cherry Port Reduction, 47
    Coconut Pecan Bonbons, 59
    Cream Puffs with Cinnamon

Chocolate Whipped Cream, 51
    Earl Grey Chocolate Mousse, 54
    Espresso Brownies, 31
    Heavenly Trifle, 57
    Holy Habanero Fudge, 60
    Marbled Double Chocolate Chip Cookies, 28
    Truffles, 62
Double Chocolate Cherry Muffins, 23
Earl Grey Chocolate Mousse, 54
Empanadas, Chocolate Pumpkin, 27
entrees
    Chile-Rubbed Steaks, 35
    Pecan Chile Chicken, 33
    Smokin' Hot Chili, 34
    Turkey Mole, 36
Espresso Brownies, 31
French Toast, Chocolate Stuffed, with Orange Marmalade Sauce, 22
Frozen Chocolate Orange Mousse, 67
frozen dishes
    Adobe Mud Pie, 65
    Caramel Mocha Shake, 69
    Chocolate Cherries Jubilee, 63
    Chocolate Chile Ice Cream, 66
    Frozen Chocolate Orange Mousse, 67
    Helado Azteca, 66
    Profiteroles, 64
    Super Chocolaty Chocolate Shake, 69
Fudge, Holy Habanero, 60
Ganache, Basic, 15
gianduia
    Chocolate Burritos, 25
    Chocolate Pizza, 25
    Gianduia Puff Pastry, 21
Grilled Chocolate–Peanut-Butter Sandwiches, 26
habanero chile powder
    Holy Habanero Fudge, 60
Heavenly Trifle, 57
Helado Azteca, 66
Holy Habanero Fudge, 60

hot chocolate
  Almond Joy Hot Chocolate,   71
  Captain Jack's Hot Chocolate,   73
  On-the-Go Cocoa Mix,   71
  Traditional Mexican Hot Chocolate,   70
ice cream (*see also shake*)
  Chocolate Chile Ice Cream,   66
  Helado Azteca,   66
Marbled Double Chocolate Chip Cookies,   28
Mexican chocolate
  Champurrado,   70
  Traditional Mexican Hot Chocolate,   70
  Turkey Mole,   36
Mocha Buzz,   72
Mole, Turkey,   36
Molten Chocolate Cakes,   45
Mousse, Earl Grey Chocolate,   54
Mousse, Frozen Chocolate Orange,   67
Mud Pie, Adobe,   65
Muffins, Double Chocolate Cherry,   23
On-the-Go Cocoa Mix,   71
Orange Mocha,   72
Pancakes, Chocolate Chip Pecan,   18
Panna Cotta, Chocolate Mint,   49
pasilla chile powder
  Turkey Mole,   36
Pecan Chile Chicken,   33

Profiteroles,   64
pudding
  Arroz con Leche y Chocolate,   46
  Chocolate Bread Pudding with Cinnamon Crème Anglaise,   52
  Chocolate Natillas,   56
  Chocolate Rice Pudding,   46
Rice Pudding, Chocolate,   46
Sauce, Basic Chocolate,   15
semisweet chocolate (*see bittersweet chocolate*)
Shake, Caramel Mocha,   69
Shake, Super Chocolaty Chocolate,   69
Smokin' Hot Chili,   34
snacks
  Chocolate Burritos,   25
  Chocolate Pizza,   25
  Grilled Chocolate–Peanut-Butter Sandwiches,   26
Steaks, Chile-Rubbed,   35
Super Chocolaty Chocolate Shake,   69
Syrup, Basic Chocolate,   16
toasting nuts,   13
Toffee, Almond,   61
Traditional Mexican Hot Chocolate,   70
Truffles,   62
Turkey Mole,   36
white chocolate,   12
  Chocolate Pizza,   25